Edward Bicknell

The territorial acquisitions of the United States

A historical review

Edward Bicknell

The territorial acquisitions of the United States
A historical review

ISBN/EAN: 9783337185367

Printed in Europe, USA, Canada, Australia, Japan

Cover: Foto ©ninafisch / pixelio.de

More available books at **www.hansebooks.com**

THE
Territorial Acquisitions of the United States

An Historical Review
BY
EDWARD BICKNELL

BOSTON
SMALL, MAYNARD & COMPANY
1899

Press of
George H. Ellis, Boston, U.S.A.

PREFACE

Because all the world is discussing the results of the war of 1898, this historical review, which recites in detail all the precedents established by the United States since the beginning of its government, should aid very greatly the intelligent comprehension of the subject.

It is evidently the author's intention to avoid partisanship or controversy. He has told the whole truth, in simple graphic language, concerning every event that has occurred which has any relation to the gradual growth of a small, scattered group of States into the magnificent domain which is now the United States of America; and he has left the reader to his own conclusions as to the propriety and wisdom of extending the national control to lands beyond the sea.

W.

CONTENTS

Chapter I. The Northwestern Territory. 1787 . . . . Page 3

Extent of the thirteen original States — The Northwestern Territory the first national domain — Organized before the adoption of the Constitution — An additional bond of union and an incentive to a needed national feeling — Its organization the foundation of our system of territorial government — Slavery within it forbidden, but tacitly permitted south of the Ohio — To be held under territorial government only temporarily — The same theory in regard to all the territories until 1898.

Chapter II. Louisiana. 1802 . . Page 11

First acquisition of foreign land — The Louisiana Purchase — The region explored and occupied first by the French — La Salle — Ceded to Spain in compensation for land lost by her in aiding France — Early quarrels between the United States and Spain — Navigation of the Mississippi in question — Its importance to the Western country — The treaty with Spain under Washington's administration — Difficulties created by Spain in John Adams's administration — Spain's agreement to restore Louisiana to France — French possession a political and commercial danger to the United States.

Chapter III. Louisiana (concluded) Page 21

Jefferson's position — Monroe and Livingston exceed their authority and grasp the great opportunity — Treaty made selling Louisiana to the United States — Its further provision that States

CONTENTS

should in time be formed from the territory ceded — The opposition of the Federalists — Their allegations as to the incompatibility of the population with our institutions and the unconstitutionality of the annexation — The treaty ratified, however, with little effective opposition — Prophecies of ills to follow not fulfilled — No especial benefit to the South more than to the North — Free States as well as slave States formed within the territory — The Constitution stretched, but not amended — First precedent as to the power of annexation established — Consent of people not deemed necessary, another precedent.

Chapter IV. Florida. 1819 . . Page 31

Owned by Spain — Ceded to England and then restored to Spain — West Florida "annexed" to the Union — Another step in the development of the power of the national government — Jackson's invasion in 1814 — Our possession in 1818 — Troubles with the Seminoles — Jackson's second invasion — The whole territory finally bought by the United States under a species of duress — Boundary line between Mexico (Spanish) and the United States fixed at same time — Little question as to the constitutional power to acquire Florida — The Louisiana precedent strengthened — Louisiana and Florida a benefit to the whole Union.

Chapter V. Oregon. 1846 . . Page 40

Acquired through discovery and by occupation — The fur trade — Captain Gray and the Columbia — Jefferson's encouragement — Lewis and Clark's expedition — John Jacob Astor's enterprise — Dispute with England — The "Oregon Question" in politics — "Fifty-four forty or fight" — Convention with England concluded — Boundary fixed by compromise.

CONTENTS

Chapter VI. Texas. 1845 . . Page 50

Slavery potent in the acquisition of territory from Mexico — Early occupation by the Spanish of what is now our Southwest — Less conspicuous in Texas — Contraband trade — Dissatisfaction in the United States with the boundary line fixed in 1819 — Henry Clay's opposition.

Chapter VII. Texas (concluded) . Page 56

Mexican independence gained — Stephen F. Austin — Early settlers of Texas — Texas joined in one Mexican State with Coahuila — Injustice of the Mexican authorities — Texas American in its people and habits of thought — Two attempts on the part of the United States to buy Texas from Mexico — Texas petitions the Mexican government to be allowed to become a separate Mexican State — Revolts from Mexico — Sam Houston's victory — Texas independent — Polk's election — Annexed to the United States by joint resolution — Annexation not to be condemned *per se*, but because of manner and time — Clay's views.

Chapter VIII. The Mexican Cessions. 1848; 1853 . . . . . Page 67

The Mexican War — Apparently a war of conquest — Santa Anna — The Wilmot Proviso — Scott's victory — A large amount of territory ceded to the United States by the Treaty of Peace, and compensation given to Mexico — States to be formed from the ceded territory — The party responsible for the war defeated at the next national election — The Gadsden purchase — Last acquisition of contiguous territory by the United States — Results of the Mexican War — Beginning of the end of slavery — Texas the last slave State admitted to the Union.

CONTENTS

Chapter IX. Alaska. 1867 . . Page 75

Its purchase from Russia — Commercial reasons govern the annexation — Not contiguous to the United States — A new precedent established — Consent of its people dispensed with as in previous cases except Texas — Expectation that it would remain under permanent territorial government — Such government practically that of a colony or province — Another precedent thus established — The discovery and occupation by Russia — American interests — Fisheries — Mineral wealth — Ceded to the United States — No opposition to the treaty — Treaty rights of civilized inhabitants — Acquisitions of to-day different in character from any before.

Chapter X. Hawaii. 1898 . . Page 83

Annexation of Hawaii justified on naval grounds or to protect American interests paramount in the islands — Its people — Early history — The Kamehameha dynasty — Treaty with the United States in 1874 — American capital invested in the islands and the American colony there — Revolution of 1887 — Suffrage extended to aliens — Accession of Liliuokalani — Schemes for annexation — Sympathy of the United States minister with the movement.

Chapter XI. Hawaii (concluded) . Page 92

Queen proposes a new constitution — Committee of Safety formed — Monarchical system of government abrogated and queen deposed — Annexation to the United States proposed — Action of United States marines — Treaty of annexation laid before the Senate by President Harrison — Withdrawn by President Cleveland — His action in the matter — The Republic of Hawaii proclaimed — An-

CONTENTS

other treaty of annexation proposed by President McKinley — Effect of our war with Spain upon annexation — A new thought — Annexation finally accomplished by joint resolution — Course of our government not to be viewed with complacency, whatever the results.

Chapter XII. Conclusion . . . Page 100

The recent acquisitions in the West Indies and the East — Result of a review of our past acquisitions: precedents made allowing our government to extend the boundaries of the country wherever it deems it proper so to do — The story not all creditable — Action through ignorance of facts at the time — Precedents allowing annexation unquestionably having been made, shall we limit our power? — The government of territories wherever situated or however peopled a trust which cannot be evaded.

Appendix . . . . Page 106

THE
TERRITORIAL ACQUISITIONS
OF THE UNITED STATES

CHAPTER I.
THE NORTHWESTERN TERRITORY.

WHEN England recognised the independence of the United States of America, and treated them as "free, sovereign, and independent States," those States occupied a territory extending, roughly speaking, from the Great Lakes at the north to the 31st parallel of north latitude, or about fifty miles north of the Gulf of Mexico, at the south; and from the Atlantic to the Mississippi. All the rest of the country embraced in the United States of to-day south of British Columbia was then practically Spanish territory, mostly unexplored and unknown. To-day, in addition to Alaska and Hawaii and the more recent possessions, the United States of America extends quite to the Gulf of Mexico on the south, and to the Pacific on the west; and every foot of the increase of territory, except the Oregon country and Texas, has been gained through a cession from some foreign power, with no great amount of inquiry as to the consent of the inhabitants of the territory thus acquired.

TERRITORIAL ACQUISITIONS

The United States began to acquire national territory of its own, as distinct from the ownership of the individual States, very early in its career, by absorbing the Northwestern Territory, so called. Before the Constitution was adopted and while the States were bound together by the Confederation, under which they fought out the Revolutionary War, but which was so weak as barely to survive it, the beginning of a national domain was made. The settled portions of the States were, broadly speaking, along the Atlantic east of the Alleghanies; and between these portions of the States and the Mississippi there was a comparatively large and certainly rich country, which was claimed by several of the States.

The charters under which some of the Colonies, subsequently States, claimed their land, carried their respective boundaries at least to the Mississippi, so far as the English title extended; but owing to carelessness or lack of geographical knowledge when the charters were made, and the little comparative value of the unsettled wilderness, there were a duplication of grants and a confusion about them which made the titles of the western portions, still unsettled, ob-

NORTHWESTERN TERRITORY

scure, doubtful, and conflicting. These western lands were constant sources of irritation, and bade fair to involve the new nation in disastrous domestic difficulties. They also worked an injustice toward such States as had no such western lands. The States having land outside of their own proper domains had property from which to reimburse themselves for the losses incurred in gaining independence, while the other States had no such resources; and yet all had borne, in a greater or less degree, the pains, hardships, and losses of the struggle.

To end the possibility of domestic dissensions arising out of conflicting claims, and especially to give the Confederation some property from which to pay its running expenses and the debts incurred in the war waged for the benefit of all, the various States claiming such lands, at different times, ceded to the United States these western lands; and so in this way the national government became a land-owner. The land north of the Ohio, known as the Northwestern Territory and comprising the present States of Ohio, Indiana, Illinois, Wisconsin, Michigan, and part of Minnesota, came into the hands of the United States

TERRITORIAL ACQUISITIONS

between 1780 and 1786. The land south of the Ohio was not ceded to the United States until later; but by 1802 the government held what is now Mississippi and Alabama (except a strip across the southern part of them owned by Spain) as a territory, while Kentucky and Tennessee, which had been ceded by Virginia and North Carolina, had been admitted as States.

No more important domestic occurrence marked our early history than the cession to the United States of the land comprising the Northwestern Territory. The Union was at that time in the greatest danger of falling to pieces. The Confederation had served to carry the States through the war. The common cause and common danger had acted to hold them together; but, when peace came, the strain seemed almost too much for the weak bonds of confederation. Local jealousies, quarrels about territory, commercial conflicts between the States, the poverty and confusion occasioned by war, and the lack of a national feeling shown through the war itself,— all combined to give color to the prophecy of Europeans, that the Union must soon dissolve through internal dissensions. Moreover, Congress was obliged

NORTHWESTERN TERRITORY

continually to press the States for money, to remind them of their obligations. There was not enough of active honesty and patriotism left after the war to urge a prompt performance of their duties to the Union, however careful the States might be to look out for their own immediate and individual interests. The people were apt to think first of their respective States, not of the Union. They had struggled continuously for many years, had been through an eight years' war, with all the anxieties and deprivations which that implies; and it needed a very sturdy patriotism and a very deep-rooted virtue, widely diffused, to keep up the struggle after the outside pressure was removed. The country was in the same state of weakness, with the same low vitality, in which a man finds himself after a high fever. But when the Union, by gaining this valuable tract of territory, possessed a national domain,— a territory which, thrown open to immigration, would pay the cost of the entire war,— less than ever would it need to call upon the States for money. It possessed something in which every State had an interest, something which nourished that national feeling and pride so sorely needed.

TERRITORIAL ACQUISITIONS

It was a territory which meant very much to the people of the United States. It was within it that France had tried to gain a foothold, and, by drawing a chain of settlements and fortified posts around the English Colonies, to stifle them or drive them into the sea. As the Colonies grew in population, and there were fewer openings at home for the adventurous and colonising spirit of our fathers, it was to this territory along the Ohio and down the Mississippi that they turned their eyes and gave their thoughts. It was the efforts made for its possession by the French and English which began the last and decisive French war in this country. It was to gain a clear title to it that the Colonies had contributed their blood and their treasure, and the victory gained at the fall of New France was theirs as well as England's. And it was this same Northwestern Territory which the skill and bravery of George Rogers Clark and his company had conquered in the Revolutionary War after the British had taken possession, and which was saved to us when the treaty of peace was made in 1783 only by skilful diplomacy.

So when all this Northwestern Territory, the land north of the Ohio, became a

NORTHWESTERN TERRITORY

national domain, the new nation had something in which the people had an interest outside of their own particular States. It was one bond of union at a time when the old bonds were loosening. The famous Ordinance of 1787, by which this territory was organised and governed, formed the model for governing the territories afterward acquired. It was the beginning, and it laid the foundation for our system of territorial government. In the light of after events, perhaps the most important provision in the ordinance was the prohibition of slavery within the territory. Thus it came about that the States formed within that section of our country were free States at their beginning.

The Constitution went into effect in 1789, and our government as it is to-day came into being. To the Union under its new establishment Georgia and North Carolina ceded their western lands, and in framing measures for the government of these new territories the main provisions of the Ordinance of 1787 were followed, except that slavery was not forbidden.

Up to this time the United States possessed territory only which had been surrendered to

TERRITORIAL ACQUISITIONS

it by the States. The national domain was common property contributed by the States themselves, which did not add to the area of the United States taken as a whole. This land, surrendered to the United States, plainly was to be held under territorial government only until it developed sufficiently to be fit for local State government. All the acts of Congress and every measure relating to it show this. Every other acquisition since has been of foreign territory; but, like the North-western Territory, these acquisitions, down to that of Alaska, have been domains contiguous to the States then existing, and fitted by the population, which would naturally flow into them, to become like the older States in their people and habits of government and thought. It was the natural expectation and intention of our people, stipulated in all the treaties of annexation until that of Alaska, that these districts temporarily held under territorial government should eventually become States. That idea has been connected with all our acquisitions down to the time of the purchase of Alaska.

CHAPTER II.

LOUISIANA.

When the United States under its new form of government was fairly started, it began to grow in territory as well as in other wealth. It then began to acquire foreign land. The question of the constitutionality of such acquisitions was raised at the outset; but the first annexation was made notwithstanding, and the validity of the act has never been overruled.

The purchase of Louisiana, our first acquisition of foreign territory, grew out of the situation of the States, and of the necessity for a seaport for the Northwestern Territory and the Mississippi Territory and the States already formed in that section of the country. These reasons, and the situation of the political parties at that time, prevented any effective opposition to the transaction.

Louisiana was the name given by the French to the region drained by the Mississippi and its tributaries. The territory embraced extended from the Alleghanies to the Rocky Mountains. France claimed all of it by a title of discovery and occupation,

TERRITORIAL ACQUISITIONS

alleging the exploration of the Mississippi to its mouth, and the French settlements made from New Orleans to Canada. The prior discovery of De Soto had passed out of mind, or at any rate had not been followed by occupation, when La Salle, the Frenchman, and one of the greatest of the early heroes of this country, with a perseverance and endurance never excelled, after repeated trials, thwarted by temporary failure and by embarrassments of every kind, sailed along the Great Lakes, penetrated the wilderness to the Illinois River, then journeyed down that river to the Mississippi, and down the Mississippi to the Gulf of Mexico. His magnificent scheme of military and trading posts along the great waterway, of alliances with the Indians, of forming a power which would check the Spanish in an advance from Mexico, and bind the English to their posts east of the Alleghanies, he did not live to put in practice himself; and, fortunately for England and ourselves, it was only entered upon when the great struggle between France and England for the possession of this country began. After seventy-four years of almost continual warfare the French were overcome.

LOUISIANA

When the end came, and France was obliged to strip herself of her American possessions, she released to England, in addition to Canada, the country east of the Mississippi down to the Spanish possession of Florida. The vast domain west of the Mississippi she gave to Spain to repay that power for what it had lost in the fight; for, in the last years of the struggle, Spain had come to the aid of France, and had been bereft of some of her own territory as well.

So Spain succeeded to the French title to Louisiana, which name was now confined to the land west of the river. A few Spanish settlements sprang up in this region, but there was no such vigour in Spanish colonising as to leave any lasting impression. The change was not acceptable to the citizens of New Orleans, who were French in blood and remained so in sympathy.

Meanwhile the English Colonies grew apace. Settlers began to penetrate in increasing numbers through the Alleghanies into the fertile country of the Ohio and the northwest. Kentucky became settled in a measure. Tennessee began to upbuild. The United States came into being; and the new nation, with all the energy of youth, was

TERRITORIAL ACQUISITIONS

stretching toward the Mississippi, and looking longingly down the river to the Gulf. Spain, in the spirit of monopoly, common enough in that age, or fearing for her other possessions along the Gulf, at first tried to restrict the navigation of the Mississippi to her own people, while the whole of the United States along the Mississippi and Ohio felt shut in without the outlet which nature had put at its feet. The free navigation of the Mississippi was a burning question to citizens of Ohio and Kentucky and the then western part of our country. While Spain held New Orleans, there was bound to be trouble unless restrictions on the commerce of the river were removed. For Spain then held the territory on both sides of the river, and the United States nowhere touched the Gulf; Florida, which in those days extended from the Atlantic to the Mississippi, having been returned to Spanish authority after only a short English possession.

In the latter days of the Confederation and in the early days of our republic, Spain was an uncomfortable neighbour; and Washington's administration continued to be full of difficulties with her over the northern boundary of Florida and the navigation of

LOUISIANA

the Mississippi. She refused to allow the free navigation of the river until the boundary dispute was settled. The people of our then western section were not slow in expressing their feelings upon the situation. At various times Spain tried to foment dissensions between Kentucky and Tennessee and the rest of the Union; but, although she failed to bring about a separation, her acts drove the western settlers to the President and Congress with passionate remonstrances. The opinion was openly expressed that there was opposition between the eastern and western parts of the country, and that the attempts of our government to open the river had been feeble and insincere; and there were some grounds upon which to base such an opinion. The western men claimed as a merit that they had so long abstained from using the means they possessed for the assertion of "a natural and inalienable right." Such demonstrations of feeling seemed sure to bring us into hostilities with Spain, if they did not kindle difficulties among ourselves; and Spain's alliance with England made her very positive and arrogant in tone. But at length, in 1795, Washington's administration managed to conclude a treaty with Spain

TERRITORIAL ACQUISITIONS

which nominally settled the boundary dispute and threw open the Mississippi to free navigation, and also gave the people of the United States the privilege of depositing merchandise for transshipment in New Orleans, or some other designated port on the river near there, free of duty. While Spain was not very prompt in observing the boundaries laid down in this treaty, the Mississippi problem was settled for the time being. After that the relations of the United States with Spain were fairly friendly, except once when, in John Adams's administration, the right of deposit was interdicted. The President had determined to compel Spain to open a depot for American trade in accordance with the treaty, when the right of deposit was restored, whereupon everything was again serene. This state of things continued till 1802.

In that year it became known that in 1800 France had made a secret treaty with Spain under which Louisiana was to be restored to France upon certain conditions since fulfilled. Napoleon was then Consul, and, with the rest of his contemporaries, shared an ambition for distant possessions, for colonies whose trade he might monopo-

LOUISIANA

lise. Egypt was, even then, a rather uncertain possession. Louisiana, with its vast extent and its natural resources, having formerly belonged to France, the pride of France would be gratified by its return. It would give Napoleon a foothold in America, the control, as he believed and intended, of the commerce of the Great River, with possibilities in the future hardly to be realised.

Napoleon had no trouble in bringing Spain to his wishes. He had become too strong to have difficulties raised by that country, and so the treaty was made. In 1802, having fulfilled his part of the agreement, Napoleon got ready to take possession of his American acquisitions. He assembled his vessels and troops, and made some negotiations to obtain Florida also: then he had to wait awhile. The indiscretion of the Spanish officials allowed the particulars of these negotiations to reach the English ambassador, whereupon British jealousy at once took alarm and raised a mass of obstacles. So, in 1803, he found himself still without possession of Louisiana and on the eve of war with Great Britain. In the event of war at that time Louisiana was vulnerable. To say nothing of what the United

TERRITORIAL ACQUISITIONS

States might be tempted to undertake, England would surely strike there; for not a French soldier was on American soil, and hardly one could be spared from other quarters. A message from George III. to his Parliament, showing preparations for war, dispelled all the colonial dreams of the First Consul. It became then his object to dispose of Louisiana to the best advantage. Selling it to the United States would help him to some needed money and do an ill turn to England. It not only would make the United States a little more friendly, perhaps, but would make it a power which might threaten England's American possessions, and, as he said, a maritime rival which would sooner or later humble England's pride.

The Consul very easily came to arrangements with the United States. Much as its people disliked to have Spain at the mouth of the Mississippi, they felt that it would be worse to have a strong power like France there, especially in view of what seemed to be her proposed policy. French forces sent to Hayti were believed by many to be destined ultimately for Louisiana, to maintain French dominion supreme there

LOUISIANA

and extend it if possible. In 1802, acting under French influence, Spain again closed New Orleans as a place of deposit. This virtually closed the Mississippi to the people of the United States, and was a sample of what might be expected when Napoleon should get possession.

When this action of Spain became known, and the people of Kentucky and of the western States and territories began to feel the results of this unfriendly policy, and trade down the river ceased, the pressure upon the administration to take aggressive measures became almost too strong to be withstood. The Federalists taunted Jefferson with cowardice. It seemed difficult for them to find words to express their disgust at his lack of action. Perhaps they took this attitude for political reasons, hoping to gain western support; but we should prefer to believe an honest patriotism moved them. The Mississippi difficulty was no new thing, as we have seen. Washington had only averted a possible secession of the western States, or war with Spain, by the treaty of 1795, and John Adams stopped at force only because Spain yielded. So the Federalists, not having now the responsibility of the

TERRITORIAL ACQUISITIONS

government on their shoulders, might well urge the most vigourous measures. Besides, party feeling was high and unreasonable; and many a Federalist honestly believed that Jefferson and his party were under French influence and ready to cater to Napoleon's wishes. But war did not coincide with Jefferson's policy. Yet, "always a patriot and always intensely partisan," as he was, he was fully sensible of the fact that the presence of the French in New Orleans was perilous to his country as well as to his party. It was the popular sympathy with the French republic, and the bitter aversion to England, which was one factor in the overthrow of the Federalists, who were looked upon by many as being too fond of aristocratic and even monarchical ideas. If France held New Orleans, there was every reason to believe that she soon would be an object of bitter detestation, and the English party here would be in the ascendant. That, apparently, meant ruin to Jefferson's party. The country had not yet become emancipated from European politics, and party policies here turned very much upon the question of favouring England or France.

CHAPTER III.

LOUISIANA (Concluded).

But beyond merely a question of party success or failure there was great danger in the proposed French occupation. Jefferson writes as follows to Livingston, our minister to France: "The cession of Louisiana . . . by Spain to France works most sorely on the United States. . . . It completely reverses all the political relations of the United States, and will form a new epoch in our political course." And he goes on to speak of France as our natural friend, "as one with which we could never have an occasion of difference. Her growth, therefore," he writes, "we viewed as our own, her misfortunes ours. There is on the globe one single spot, the possessor of which is our natural and habitual enemy. It is New Orleans, through which the produce of three-eighths of our territory must pass to market; and from its fertility it will erelong yield more than half of our whole produce, and contain more than half of our inhabitants. France, placing herself in that door, assumes to us the attitude of defiance. Spain might have retained it quietly for years. Her pacific dispositions, her feeble state, would induce her to increase our facilities there, so that her possession of the place would be hardly felt by us; and it would not, perhaps, be very long before some circumstances might arise which would make the cession of it to us as the price of something of more worth to her. Not so can it ever be in the hands of France. The impetuosity of her temper, the energy and restlessness of her character, placed in a point of eternal friction with us and our character, which, though quiet and loving peace and the pursuit of wealth, is high-minded, despising wealth in competition with insult or injury, enterprising and energetic as any nation on earth,— these circumstances render it impossible that France and the United States can continue long friends when they meet in so irritable a position." And, certainly, it appeared very ominous to peace when Spain, plainly under French influence, interdicted the right of deposit at New Orleans. It looked very much as if Napoleon was trying to get possession of Louisiana unfettered by any question of treaty obligations entered into by Spain, and that he did not propose to succeed to a condition of affairs brought into being by such a treaty.

LOUISIANA

In addition to all these objections there was another, and a most grave one, to the possession or acquisition of Louisiana by France. It meant almost certainly the conquest of that province by England. With England north of the United States, and on its west, and in control of the Mississippi, the United States would be forced into an alliance with her or else into a bitter struggle, the end of which would be impossible to foresee. So it appeared that the only way out of the difficulty was for the United States to possess Louisiana for herself.

Accordingly, when Jefferson learned of the French treaty with Spain, and was informed of the closing of New Orleans to our merchants, aware, too, of the gathering war-clouds in Europe, he saw his opportunity. He made Livingston, who was already on the ground, and James Monroe, ministers plenipotentiary to purchase the Island of New Orleans, as the district around that city was called. At a little earlier date, when Livingston had presented a memorial respecting the wishes of the United States as to the navigation of the Mississippi and the acquisition of New Orleans, Napoleon had paid little attention to his representations and

TERRITORIAL ACQUISITIONS

offers. It was at that time that he had his own purposes to serve, and Louisiana and its trade were wanted for France. When, however, as we have seen, war with England became imminent, his purposes changed. Instead of accepting an offer to buy New Orleans or to arrange a treaty allowing us the privileges held under Spanish agreement, he expressed a desire to sell the whole of Louisiana. Monroe had now arrived in Paris, and no time was lost in coming to terms. Although the envoys had no authority to buy more than New Orleans, they perceived the benefit which the acquisition of the whole of Louisiana would give the United States. So a treaty was promptly arranged, to be ratified by the respective nations, by which Louisiana was ceded to the United States for about $15,000,000.

The territory thus ceded was that released to France by Spain, with its northern and western boundaries indefinite and very elastic. The boundary between Louisiana and Spanish Mexico was not defined until 1819, when the river Sabine was so designated.

The treaty stipulated that the inhabitants of Louisiana "should be incorporated into

LOUISIANA

the Union of the United States, and admitted, as soon as possible, according to the principles of the Federal Constitution, to the enjoyment of all the rights, advantages, and immunities of citizens of the United States. And in the mean time they should be maintained and protected in the free enjoyment of their liberty, property, and the religion which they professed." The acquisition carried the United States to the Rocky Mountains, or, if Oregon was included, as has been claimed, to the Pacific Ocean; and the region contained a population of eighty thousand, of which half were slaves. The larger part of this population was, of course, in or about New Orleans.

Napoleon soon ratified the treaty on the part of France, and Jefferson, with a natural satisfaction, at once communicated the facts to Congress and laid the treaty before it for ratification and the necessary legislation. He hinted at the possible necessity of a constitutional amendment, but he advised his friends to say very little on that point.

The annexation naturally met with a bitter opposition from the Federalists, and some of Jefferson's own party doubted its wisdom; but the mass of the people, partic-

TERRITORIAL ACQUISITIONS

ularly those of the south and west, heartily approved it. The opposition said that "the acquiring territory with money is mean and despicable." It held that Louisiana was a wilderness of little value, while the population was slightingly spoken of as a "*Gallo-Hispano-Indian omnium gatherum* of savages and adventurers, whose pure morals are expected to sustain and glorify our republic." The opposition could not believe that such a class of population was suited to a republican form of government, and it did not seem to think of or believe in immigration of our people. As a matter of fact, neither party appreciated the real value of the purchase. Again, the Federalists opposed the annexation because the addition of so much new western and southern territory would give such an undue predominance to southern ideas and institutions as to threaten the destruction of the political influence of the northern and eastern States. Besides the insinuation that Jefferson simply took this method of helping France with a little ready money when it was badly needed by her, the Federalists denied the constitutionality of the measure, although they as a party, especially when in power, so construed the Constitution

LOUISIANA

as to give the government the largest implied powers. The anti-Federalists, or, more properly at this time, the Democratic-Republican party, believed in limiting those powers; but, when it got control of the government and felt its responsibilities, it also became more general in its policy, and favoured the annexation. So, in spite of all opposition, especially since the Federalists were weak in numbers in the Senate, the treaty was ratified, the legislation to carry it into effect passed, and Louisiana became a part of the United States.

The Federalists prophesied all manner of evil from this result. Fisher Ames writes to Christopher Gore in October, 1803: " The Mississippi was a boundary somewhat like Governor Bowdoin's whimsical all-surrounding orb — we were confined within some limits. Now, by adding our unmeasured world beyond that river, we rush like a comet into infinite space. In our wild career we may jostle some other world out of its orbit; but we shall, in every event, quench the light of our own." But the dangers foretold were not realised. Free States, as well as slave States, grew out of Louisiana. New England more than the south occupied the

TERRITORIAL ACQUISITIONS

vacant western lands, and the wealth and prosperity of the great West has come to us by reason of this extension of our boundaries beyond the Mississippi.

It has been remarked that Jefferson and some of his party leaders doubted the constitutional right of annexation. An amendment to the Constitution authorising it was prepared, but was never submitted to the States. The measure was acquiesced in as lying within the treaty powers of the President and Senate, or being within the general powers of government, or perhaps as within the power of admitting new States to the Union. The party to which Jefferson belonged was the party of a strict construction of the Constitution. It believed in limiting the powers of the general government as much as possible and still allow the government to exist. Yet at its first entrance into control it carried the sovereignty of the national government as far as the Federalists had ever done. "The acquisition of Louisiana was an immense help in bringing about just that which" Jefferson and his party had opposed, "the subordination of the State to the Nation." That step was ratified by Congress, and stands as a precedent to-day.

LOUISIANA

It was thus a matter of the gravest importance to us, irrespective of the material wealth it brought to the country, in its effect upon the question of the constitutional power of the United States to annex contiguous territory without the consent of the people of that territory. It is difficult to see, if our government has the power thus to annex contiguous territory, why it may not for the same reasons annex territory anywhere. The remoteness of a proposed acquisition, the character of its people, are questions which affect the desirability of annexation, and not the power, if the Louisiana precedent be accepted.

Since the treaty with France provided that the inhabitants of Louisiana should be "incorporated into the Union," or, in other words, that States should be formed out of it as soon as possible, according to the provisions of the Federal Constitution, this new acquisition, like the territories hitherto belonging to the Union, was held under a trust, as it were, to form States when proper. Perhaps the Louisiana case goes no further as a precedent than that, under a construction of the Constitution adopted by the President and Congress and acquiesced in by the people

TERRITORIAL ACQUISITIONS

(and, as we shall see, subsequently followed), the United States has the power to annex territory out of which States are to be formed. It fairly may be said that at that time the power of the United States under the Constitution to hold colonies or dependencies which were not intended to be made into States, and ultimately to have a voice and a vote in our legislative assemblies and in the election of our national officers, was not considered. That may be said to have been left an open question.

CHAPTER IV.

FLORIDA.

FLORIDA presented some of the same aspects from the point of view of the United States as Louisiana. It was a province which had always seemed to furnish a base of operations against the peace and quietness of the people in the Southern States as well as a constant temptation to invasion. Spain was a weak power, and neither preserved order in Florida nor could protect it when citizens of the United States were the aggressors. Discovered by Spain in 1513 and its first town built in 1565, she established only a few settlements within it; and the greater part of its territory still remained occupied only by Indians until 1763, when Spain ceded it to England in exchange for Cuba which England had taken in the war just ended. It was assumed to extend from the Atlantic to the Mississippi, with the northern boundary unsettled. England divided it into East and West Florida, with the Appalachicola as the dividing line. When she made peace with the United States, in 1783, she also made a treaty with Spain by which

TERRITORIAL ACQUISITIONS

Florida was returned to its former owner. Then a good many settlers from the United States, who had gone there through English inducements while it was under English government, returned to this country. The northern boundary still remained unsettled until it was fixed by the treaty already mentioned, in 1795, at a line running along the thirty-first parallel from the Mississippi to the Chattahoochee, then down that river to Flint River, and then across to the head waters of St. Mary's River. Very slowly and reluctantly Spain withdrew her forces south of that line.

The United States began her serious encroachments upon Florida in 1810, when, taking advantage of an insurrection of West Florida against Spanish authority, the federal government took possession of some of the principal posts west of the Perdido River, and soon after annexed the part on the east bank of the Mississippi to the territory of Orleans (the southern part of the Louisiana Purchase). The people of West Florida had proposed, when they revolted from Spain, to become annexed to the United States; but our government seemed to prefer the course taken, leaving the title to negotiation. In

FLORIDA

spite of the treaty of 1795 fixing the northern boundary, the people on the United States side seemed to feel that they had a claim to the country west of the Perdido, relying upon the claim of France to that district when she held Louisiana. Above all, the action taken gave us land on both sides of the Mississippi. That may have been sufficient for the administration. The next year Congress authorised the acquisition of the entire province, if Spain would consent to it, or any other power tried to obtain it.

Very soon another slice of this land occupied by the United States was added to the Mississippi Territory, and so matters remained as far as the federal government was concerned until 1814. This occupation of West Florida gave rise to earnest debates in Congress; but the country was too much occupied with commercial difficulties and strained relations with England and France to pay the attention to the matter which it deserved. It was another step in the development of the power of the national government.

In 1814, to prevent the British, then at war with the United States, from using Pensacola as a base of supplies, and having

TERRITORIAL ACQUISITIONS

Spanish help in proposed operations against us in the South, Andrew Jackson, then a general in our army, marched against that city, and, defeating the British and Spanish defenders, took possession of it. A couple of days later, when the British were found to have left that section of the country, he restored the city to the Spanish.

While Florida was a Spanish province, there were several cases of aggression on the part of our people in the South; but in 1818 our government itself ordered an invasion, and retained possession for a time on the plea of restoring order. The state of affairs in the province was such as to invite trouble. Spain, upon regaining possession in 1783, never fully reoccupied it. Only a few small military posts here and there nominally held in check a population made up in a great measure of outlaws, smugglers, and buccaneers, while the fierce and warlike Seminoles prevented the colonisation of many of the best sections. The American occupation, in 1818, came about from the efforts of our government to disperse a band of filibusters, calling themselves patriots, who had landed on an island near the boundary of Georgia with the proclaimed intention of

FLORIDA

invading East Florida and annexing it to the United States. Practically, their presence there hindered the execution of our revenue laws. Our troops took possession of the country to hold, as our government informed Spain, until that power was able to maintain order.

Then difficulties with the Seminoles broke out. These Indians, living on both sides of the line between Florida and Georgia, had committed acts which led Georgia to complain to the government at Washington. General Jackson took the field against them, and pursued them into Florida. He himself had no doubt of the complicity of the Spanish in these Indian outrages and of their furnishing supplies to the red men, and so he proceeded to take two or three Spanish forts in Florida and to occupy Pensacola again. This time he appointed a military governor, abolished Spanish revenue laws, and, in general, proceeded in a vigourous if high-handed course. Although these proceedings caused great excitement and considerable censure, Congress passed a vote of thanks to Jackson; while the administration, after much hesitation, expressed its approbation of his acts. The people made an idol of him; and this

TERRITORIAL ACQUISITIONS

work in Florida, with his great victory over the British at New Orleans, fixed his popularity sufficiently secure to make him President ten years or so later.

Pensacola and our other captures in Florida were subsequently returned to Spain; and then, in 1819, Spain agreed to cede the whole province to us for five million dollars. The province had then only a very small population, with the whites clustered round a few settlements. The greater part was still roamed over by the native Indians.

Before Spain would make this treaty, however, she insisted upon defining the boundary between the Louisiana Purchase and Mexico, the latter then in her possession. The United States had made claims so far as the Rio Grande, while Spain allowed only a narrow strip west of the Mississippi. When the Sabine River was agreed upon as the boundary, she ceded Florida, as desired. In thus gaining Florida, we relinquished any claim we had upon what was afterwards the republic of Texas.

Spain had her hands full at the time with the continuous revolutions in her South American provinces and in Mexico, and perhaps she made this cession under a species of duress. The acts of the United States officials, particularly those of General Jackson, which had been hailed with delight in the States, had not been such as to give Spain a feeling of security in the possession of Florida; and she may have regarded the money as worth more to her, under the circumstances, than this doubtful possession. It was 1821 before she ratified the treaty and withdrew her forces. General Jackson already had been appointed governor of the new territory; and with his characteristic vigour and disregard of consequences he, in his own way, rather accelerated the departure of the Spanish officials.

The Florida question was thus settled. If the slave-owners of Southern Georgia and Alabama felt that now a refuge for their runaway property was closed, the Union as a whole could feel that one source of expense was stopped,— through its acquisition of a country which had been a constant danger to the South from the old colonial days. If Spain could not or would not maintain order there, our government could and would. This acquisition finished out the south-eastern portion of our domain, and carried our coast line unbroken from Maine to Louisiana.

Little question about the constitutional

TERRITORIAL ACQUISITIONS

power of our government to make this annexation was raised. The precedent of Louisiana was followed, and made stronger by being followed. As in the case of Louisiana, the consent of the inhabitants of the ceded territory was not asked. As in that case, it was an act in which the benefit to the United States only was considered; and arrangements were made with sovereign power, not with the people governed. The inhabitants of the new territory, as we have seen, were not a particularly desirable class; yet, as in Louisiana, there was every expectation that in time it would develop to a position when it could be properly admitted to the Union as a State, as eventually it was.

The annexation of Louisiana and Florida did away with troublesome neighbours, prevented further certain irritation and perhaps war. Their acquisition was justified by the circumstances of the times and events; and, however much such additions to the southern part of the country may have helped that section and given its peculiar institution added strength, they were also of great benefit to the country at large. Whatever motives were by the opposition attributed to the administrations which secured these additions, certainly such sectional aggrandisement was not alleged by the people favouring them as the motive; and there is no evidence to warrant the belief that it actuated those most concerned. That the annexation of Louisiana and Florida dried up the sources of chronic difficulties is reason enough for the treaties with France and Spain. As to the particular benefit to the South of the acquisition of Florida, outside of its addition as one more southern State, the most that can be said is that it helped the slave States by shutting up what had hitherto been an open door of escape for the slave. And as to Louisiana, if its acquisition did add to the slave-owning States, it also opened the Mississippi to the North, and in so doing made the free States of the Northwest the richer and more powerful.

We come now to annexation, which hardly can stand careful scrutiny as to motives and methods, however beneficial the results may have been. Before, however, treating Texas and the Mexican cession, it will be more convenient to consider the Oregon country.

CHAPTER V.

OREGON.

OREGON is the one addition to our domain which has come to us by discovery and occupation, but even then a treaty with Great Britain was required to make the title secure without possible bloodshed. Oregon also reminds us that we are a young country in the New World, for it is since the United States came into existence that white men explored the great river flowing through that territory and settled on Oregon soil.

It was the fur trade which first led us to the northwest, and it was the success of the French and the English in the north which stimulated the early interest in Oregon. As Irving has written: "While the fiery and magnificent Spaniard, inflamed with the mania for gold, has extended his discoveries and conquests over those brilliant countries scorched by the ardent sun of the tropics, the ardent and buoyant Frenchman and the cool and calculating Briton have pursued the less splendid but no less lucrative traffic in furs amidst the hyperborean regions of the Canadas, until they have advanced even

OREGON

within the arctic circle." The spirit which led "the cool and calculating Briton" into the north also caused him to cast his eyes toward the shores of the Pacific, while already his American cousin was trading for otter skins along that coast and carrying them to China for a market. With the Americans in their trading vessels on the Pacific coast, and the English working in that direction through the interior from the East, a struggle for the possession of this territory lying between Russian Alaska and Spanish California became inevitable. It was the trapper and the fur-trader who were to be the pioneers. While we would not undervalue the courage and resolution of the intrepid explorers, we should also give due meed of praise to the trappers and fur-traders who first endured the hardships and dangers of frontier life in Oregon. It was their work which carried the country's western boundary to the Pacific. They it was who led the way for the settlers who came after them. It was a repetition within the life of our nation of to-day of the trials and struggles and final success of the colonists of Massachusetts and Virginia on the Atlantic coast.

TERRITORIAL ACQUISITIONS

In 1792 Captain Gray of the ship "Columbia," of Boston, entered the Columbia River, and gave it the name of his vessel. He commanded one of those traders engaged in the fur trade along the northwest coast from California to the high northern latitudes. The coast of Oregon had been seen by many navigators before, and a large river was known to be in that vicinity; but he seems to have been the first white man who ever sailed into that river and made any exploration of it. He did not go very far up; but, as he sailed away, he met Vancouver, and, telling him of his discovery, left his charts with him. Thereupon Vancouver explored the river for a long distance from its mouth.

Captain Gray's report of his exploration upon his return home was so favourable that a desire to secure the country for the Union at once sprang up. Early in 1803 President Jefferson sent a confidential message to Congress, asking for an appropriation for an exploring expedition to the West. The appropriation was granted, and the President designated as leader of the proposed expedition Captain Meriwether Lewis. With him, as associate, was Lieutenant William

OREGON

Clark, a brother of that George Rogers Clark who had so wonderfully conquered the British in the Northwestern Territory in the Revolution.

Jefferson had for many years shown a deep interest in a proper scientific and geographical exploration of the great country west of the Alleghanies; and now, with the possible acquisition of Louisiana, and his desire for a larger knowledge of Oregon and to insure its possession by this country, he initiated this movement which resulted in Lewis and Clark's expedition. By the time they were ready to start, in 1804, Louisiana was ours, and their route lay all the way in the territory of the United States.

Lewis and Clark set out, in 1804, from the mouth of the Missouri, and sailed up the river to its sources in the Rocky Mountains, crossed the mountains to the left branch of the Columbia, and followed down that river to its mouth where Captain Gray had anchored over twelve years before. Then they returned home the way that they had come. They had passed through a country almost unknown to white men, had escaped the dangers of Indians, of snow and ice and the mountains, and the perils of unknown

TERRITORIAL ACQUISITIONS

rivers, and had brought back valuable information, besides adding another link in the chain of our title to Oregon. They were gone something over two years, and richly deserved the President's eulogy given in his message to Congress in 1806. Their story is full of adventure, and has a charm of its own quite aside from the importance of their work.

In 1810, encouraged by Jefferson, John Jacob Astor formed the Pacific Fur Company, with the object of making a settlement on the Columbia and developing the trade of that region. The company founded Astoria, and made a beginning of its work. It established a few posts along the river, and then was swallowed up by the Northwest Fur Company, its English rival in the field. The enterprise was not successful from a business point of view. When the War of 1812 broke out, Astoria and the company's goods there and at its posts were transferred to the English company, ostensibly to prevent their capture and confiscation by English troops. The evidence goes to show, however, that Astor's far-reaching and far-sighted as well as patriotic enterprise was ruined by an unfortunate selection of partners and the lack of support from our

OREGON

government. Still, the settlement at Astoria and the operations of the Pacific Fur Company were further steps and important ones in our occupation of Oregon.

After the War of 1812, in spite of a law passed by Congress forbidding British fur-traders to carry on their business upon our territory, the Northwest Fur Company continued to monopolise the trade, holding as it did posts all along the Columbia and its branches. But our people had sufficient interest in the matter to claim the whole of the country as far north as the parallel of 54° 40′, the southern limit of the Russian possessions in America. England, relying upon her occupation and alleged discovery, also claimed the territory; and, to settle the matter temporarily, an arrangement was made in 1818 for a joint occupation for the term of ten years, the people of each nation being thus authorised to trade within and occupy it. This agreement was renewed in 1827 to extend indefinitely, provided that either party might, after 1828, revoke it upon twelve months' notice.

Any possible difficulty with Russia, who owned what is now Alaska and who had established sundry trading posts in California,

TERRITORIAL ACQUISITIONS

was obviated by a treaty with her in 1824 by which she abandoned all claim to the Pacific coast south of 54° 40', the southern limit of Alaska; while Spain, at the time she ceded Florida to the United States, also released all claims to the Pacific coast north of 42°, the northern boundary of California.

The arrangement with England did very well for a time; but in 1842 the "Oregon question," which for twenty years "had been more or less before the eyes and in the thoughts of statesmen at home and abroad," received public notice in a President's message. President Tyler, in his message to Congress on Dec. 5, 1842, said: "The territory of the United States, commonly called the Oregon Territory, lying on the Pacific Ocean, north of the forty-second degree of latitude, to a portion of which Great Britain lays claim, begins to attract the attention of our fellow-citizens; and the tide of population, which has reclaimed what was so lately an unbroken wilderness in more contiguous regions, is preparing to flow over these vast districts which stretch from the Rocky Mountains to the Pacific Ocean. In the advance of the requirement of individual rights in these lands, sound policy dictates that every effort should be resorted to by the two governments to settle their respective claims." The Senate thereupon passed a bill, by a majority of one, for taking possession of the whole of the disputed territory, the title of the United States to which it was declared to be certain, and would not be abandoned. The House, however, refused to concur. The question then became a political one, with all the inflammatory appeals to national jealousy, pride, and interest which naturally might be expected under such circumstances.

When the Presidential election came round in 1844, it was one of the issues upon which Polk was elected. The cry was, "Fifty-four-forty or fight." If the Texas question was the main issue, the Oregon question added to the excitement of the times. Congressmen made fiery speeches, and the country seemed on the verge of another struggle with Great Britain, when wiser counsels prevailed; and in 1846 a convention was made by the two countries, which settled the difficulty. Monroe and Tyler had suggested a dividing line; and Polk, although elected with the understanding that he should insist upon 54° 40', made an offer of compromise; but it was not until matters had reached an acute stage that negotiations finally were concluded. It is barely possible that the Mexican difficulty rather urged Polk to a settlement with England; and it is to the credit of Daniel Webster that, although at that time he held no office in the executive department of the government, he still exerted his influence in private channels abroad to bring about a peaceful solution of the problem.

The convention made the parallel of 49° the northern boundary of Oregon, while Vancouver's Island was given to England. Free navigation of Fuca's Straits and the Columbia River was given to both nations, and rights of actual possession of land on both sides of the boundary line were to be respected by both. It was a natural boundary line, since it continued our northern boundary line directly across to the Pacific.

Thus this bone of contention between England and the United States was removed,— a contention which was aggravated by the efforts of a British company to monopolise a trade which the people of the United States felt should be theirs by right of prior occupation as well as discovery, and possibly under our construction of the Louisiana Purchase.

OREGON

This Oregon Territory is now occupied by the States of Washington, Oregon, Idaho, and parts of Montana and Wyoming. The Pacific coast line soon was extended south by the acquisition of California. So within fifty years our domain had grown from a relatively small district, confined within the Atlantic and the Mississippi, to a country extending from ocean to ocean. The steps which led to the acquisition of Texas and the Mexican territory already were being taken when Oregon became unquestionably our own.

CHAPTER VI.

TEXAS.

The annexation of Texas and the acquisition of Mexican territory adjoining it, including California, must be considered together; for they are really parts of one transaction. The acquisition of all this new territory was caused, not by extra-territorial difficulties, as in the case of Louisiana and Florida, but by a desire on the part of a portion of the country to increase its area. Although all our additions of territory thus far, except the Oregon Territory, had been at the South, at least the populous portion of them, and in the opinion of many public men gave that section so great a preponderance of influence as to endanger the Union, the demand for still further additions came from that same section. Slavery, and a desire to keep southern influence predominant in the government, were primary causes of the great additions of territory in 1845 and 1848. As the free North grew in strength, the South began to fear that, if it became strong enough to control the government, it would restrict and finally abolish

TEXAS

slavery altogether. The Missouri Compromise left only a small space for slave States; while north of 36° 20′ was an immense territory rapidly filling up with a population from New England and the North, out of which States would rise, free by the inherited principles of the settlers, and by law if the Missouri Compromise were respected. In other words, it took no prophet's eye to see a time rapidly approaching when the slave States would be in a decided minority. And just at this time a spirit of reform was rampant. It was the age of isms in New England. Prison reform, reforms in criminal law, and poor laws were agitated and undertaken; while aggressively advocated was the abolition of slavery. A period of intellectual growth and moral growth was beginning. With the denunciation of slavery *per se*, there was also a crusade begun against slavery at the South on the part of the more radical reformers. Societies for the abolition of slavery were found at the South previous to 1835; but, after that time, that section ranged itself against them, and the abolitionists were driven to the North. That party, small but earnest, would give no rest to agitation, and preferred a divided country to

TERRITORIAL ACQUISITIONS

allowing slavery protected under their flag. With this feeling springing up against slavery,— a moral feeling all the stronger from rising among a people whose very beginning was a moral struggle,— it is not strange if those at the South who believed slavery necessary to its prosperity, felt that sooner or later would come the demand for freedom for the slaves, with all its serious consequences to that section of the country. And, further, the South was in danger of losing the predominance which it had held always in the affairs of the Union; and that, especially to a State like South Carolina, was a situation not to be borne. To preserve the balance between slave and free States, more territory south of 36° 20′ must be gained. Such land was at hand in Texas.

Texas was part of that vast region in North America claimed by Spain by virtue of discovery and occupation, and was considered a part of Mexico. Spanish occupation of Texas was very limited at any time; for it was in Mexico as it is to-day, and to the north-west of Texas, that Spain made any visible progress. Before an English settler had arrived in America, little armies under Spanish leaders had penetrated into what is now

TEXAS

New Mexico and Colorado. So early as 1600 the Spanish Jesuits were exploring and establishing their missions in the more northerly and central part of the region now included in New Mexico and Arizona. Considerable success followed their efforts to Christianise the natives, a rapid emigration set in, and that district became quite flourishing. It was the reports of mineral wealth which drew these early Spanish adventurers to the wilderness. Spain always was seeking a new El Dorado, and her early expeditions to the North were to find another Mexico. With the soldier and the priest went the gold-hunter and the adventurer. But the Spaniard soon became a taskmaster. He reduced the Indians, those whom he had converted as well as others when he could, to a slavery too cruel to be borne. At last, about 1680, the natives broke into open revolt, and swept the Spanish from the country. Spain did not regain possession until eighteen years afterward.

About that time the Jesuits explored and planted missions in the country south of the Gila River. They Christianised the natives and reported the great mineral wealth there; and a large emigration from the South set in, so that a century and a quarter ago that dis-

TERRITORIAL ACQUISITIONS

trict was a thriving Spanish province. But, as usual, the Spanish enslaved the Indians; and, as had happened earlier, north of them, the slaves revolted, and killed or drove their masters from the country. Then civilisation in that section disappeared, and in 1846 only a few Mexicans remained in the old town of Tucson and along the Mesilla Valley.

There was less of Spanish occupation of Texas than of the other Spanish possessions north of Mexico. The French unwittingly made a beginning there when La Salle landed at Matagorda Bay instead of the mouth of the Mississippi, as he wished; and, after some other ineffectual attempts to establish French settlements, a French colony from the Red River located in Texas, and were allowed by the Spanish to stay there. But Spain claimed the province as part of Mexico, and practically made good her claim. When the United States bought Louisiana, only the moderation of Jefferson and the prudence of the military commanders prevented a collision of armed troops over the matter of the boundary between Mexico and this country. In 1819, however, as we have seen, the United States withdrew all claims which she had to Texas as a part of Louisiana, by the treaty fixing the Sabine River as the boundary.

TEXAS

Soon after the acquisition of Louisiana there sprang up an illicit trade with Mexico, through Texas, which was so lucrative that a large number of adventurers engaged in it. When the difficulties between Spain and her American colonies reached a point where rebellions became frequent, these adventurers, assisted by friends within the United States, made numerous attempts to free Texas and Mexico from Spanish rule; but Texan independence did not come from these efforts. The feeling which inspired these filibustering expeditions was doubtless one factor in causing the dissatisfaction displayed in the South and Southwest over the fixing of the eastern boundary of Texas in 1819. Henry Clay and other prominent men who approved that feature of the treaty expressed only a popular sentiment in their sections of the country.

CHAPTER VII.

TEXAS (Concluded).

Mexico in the mean time had been fighting for independence, and in 1821 began a revolution which ended in her freedom from Spain. During these struggles Texas lost her population, which had been of a floating character, so that by 1822 she was almost wholly deserted. In the next year, however, Stephen F. Austin received from the new nation of Mexico the confirmation of a grant of lands in Texas made by Spain in 1820 to his father, Moses Austin. Already Stephen had conducted a considerable number of colonists to a site near where the city of Austin now is, and more soon followed. The father was a native of Connecticut, but a resident of Missouri when he received his grant and began the enterprise. It was naturally the principles of Missouri and of the South which governed the early settlers. It is hardly fair to call them merely adventurers because they practically carried slavery with them, or to confuse them with their predecessors in the contraband trade which flourished there before them. Their sympathy was with slavery,

TEXAS

and probably with them were many doubtful characters; but there is little in their early history which shows them other than a set of men trying to better themselves in a new country. Later there came among them those whose object may have been simply to add to the power of the South and strengthen its institution of slavery by annexing the district to the United States. The South, in truth, favoured the colonisation of Texas, and there is good evidence of a scheme to colonise it and annex it to this country; but such a scheme was necessarily very general in its nature,— rather a strong desire than a well-defined plan. We can hardly believe that the settlement of the territory depended entirely upon the so-called conspiracy to colonise and annex it as an additional slave State. Yet, whatever part the slaveholding interest may have had in its settlement, there is no doubt that very soon after it began to grow there was a sufficiently definite purpose at the South to free it from Mexican authority, and then, if possible, to annex it to the United States. The South would not willingly allow this territory to become free from slavery, as it would if it remained Mexican, or should come under English protection or dominion, as at one time was thought possible.

When the Mexican constitution was adopted, in 1824, Texas was united with Coahuila, hitherto a separate province and one wholly Mexican, and a Mexican was placed as commandant over the department. The injustice displayed by this commandant created difficulties; but the adoption of a more liberal policy on the part of Mexico smoothed out the trouble for a few years, and Texas prospered.

Mexico, however, as we remember, was in a chronic state of revolution by that time; and in 1830 her government, then in the hands of a dictator, forbade any people from the United States entering Texas as colonists, and suspended all colony contracts which might interfere with the prohibition. From this time forward Mexican jealousy against emigrants from the United States became every month more manifest. Moreover, reckless adventurers united with the Mexican government, and went farther than it did in acts of oppression and outrage upon the colonists.

One cause of this jealousy is apparent enough. Texas was almost wholly Ameri-

TEXAS

can in population, and hardly could escape the prejudice of Mexican authorities. Then, too, many of the people of the United States felt, and expressed the feeling, that our government was all wrong in agreeing to the Sabine as the boundary with Mexico; and that we ought to have kept the whole of Texas, as it rightly, so they said, went with Louisiana. In fact, the United States tried twice in vain to buy Texas from Mexico, once under John Quincy Adams and again under Jackson. However unreasonable the views above quoted may have been, they had their weight at the South, especially since Texas was filling up with people going from our country, leaving friends and families behind, and also since Texas within our bounds would be added slave territory. Mexico had abolished slavery, and this meant that Texas would be a free country should it remain under her sovereignty. Mexico knew these facts. She knew that the citizens of Texas were aliens to Spanish or Mexican blood, and she must have felt that the bond which held that State to her was weakening every day. So in defence she took a step which, however ill-advised and unjust it may seem to us now, seemed wise to her then.

TERRITORIAL ACQUISITIONS

By 1833, the situation having become unbearable, the American settlers, who now numbered 20,000, held a convention, and determined to separate from Coahuila. A State constitution was constructed, and an address to the Mexican government prepared requesting admission to the republic as a separate State, and this at a time when Mexico herself, or the party in power there, was making the country a consolidated republic rather than a federation of States. About this time the Mexicans in Coahuila and Texas quarrelled, and each set up a different revolutionary government; but the Americans had no part in this movement. Austin went to Mexico as the agent of Texas, with the constitution and address, but could get no definite satisfaction. Santa Anna, who was then at the head of the government and wanted no separate States under him, simply played with Austin, keeping him in Mexico by promises of attention and of allowing the separate State government desired until he himself could get ready to march to Texas at the head of an army. Austin did succeed in getting the prohibition of immigration from the United States removed, and the granting of some other favour-

TEXAS

able measures; but that was all. At length he returned to Texas with the belief that only by force could anything like independence be gained for it, and that war was at hand.

In 1835, upon the report of the approach of Mexican troops, the State legislature, which had been guilty of gross frauds, was broken up and the country left without a government. The people were thus obliged either to submit to Santa Anna, in effect a dictator who already had deceived them, or form a government of their own. Being at least American born, they did not hesitate. Committees of Safety were formed, and then a provisional government; and, after a few skirmishes and battles with the Mexican troops, the latter were driven from the country. That winter a Declaration of Independence was issued; and on March 17, 1836, a convention of delegates adopted a constitution and elected officers. When Santa Anna heard of the defeat of the troops sent the year before, he himself set out for Texas at the head of an army of 7,500 men. The treacherous massacre at Goliad and the slaughter at the Alamo committed by him and his troops created a panic for a time;

TERRITORIAL ACQUISITIONS

but General Houston, the Texan commander-in-chief, drew the Mexican leader after him by a series of retreats until he reached San Jacinto. There Santa Anna's forces became divided, and Houston fell upon him, utterly routed his army, and took him prisoner. This ended the war, although neither then nor thereafter did Mexico acknowledge the independence of Texas. That new republic proposed annexation to the United States, but the latter was not then ready for it. Yet the sympathy of the American people was with the Texans in their struggle. The bloody deeds at Alamo and Goliad furnished ghastly incentives for such a feeling, and it had been shown practically by the considerable body of troops raised in the States in their aid. With all this sympathy, however, there was a conviction, especially at the North, that the South had a selfish interest in the matter.

The independence of Texas was recognised by the United States in 1837, while Mexico protested against the actions of its people. She continued to maintain a hostile attitude toward her revolted State, and sought to incite Indian forays; but she never sent another soldier against it except on one or

TEXAS

two marauding expeditions. In 1840 England, France and Belgium also recognised the independence of Texas, and the new republic began to grow rapidly. In 1843 England remonstrated against Mexico's conduct toward it; and, as a result, commissioners for an armistice were appointed. While negotiations were pending President Tyler made propositions for annexation to the United States. Texas took a little time to consider, but finally approved the project; and a treaty of annexation was made. Anxious as Tyler was to put this through, he could not carry the Senate with him; and the treaty was rejected June 8, 1844. This treaty irritated Mexico, and she broke off her negotiations, and threatened a renewal of hostilities. It displeased England and France, who wanted to see Texas under an English or joint protectorate, without slavery and free from the influence of the United States; while its rejection humiliated Texas. But Tyler's time came only a little later. Meanwhile Texas found herself burdened with debt; but her population was increasing, and by 1844 her revenues began to increase, so that she seemed to be on the road to prosperity.

TERRITORIAL ACQUISITIONS

That year the United States elections had resulted in the choice of Polk for President on a platform favoring annexation. Accordingly, in the spring of 1845 joint resolutions for annexation were passed through Congress by small majorities, were at once approved by President Tyler just before his term expired, and in July were ratified by a Texan convention called for this purpose. The population of the new State at this time was about 150,000.

Although nine years had passed since San Jacinto, and although Mexico never since had sent an army against Texas to compel submission to her, she still refused to acknowledge the independence of her former State. The action of the United States she considered an act of war against her, and her minister left Washington; but actual hostilities between the two countries did not begin at once. When they did break out, it was nominally for other reasons, as we shall see.

The annexation of Texas, in the light of her history, can hardly be condemned *per se*. It was bound to come at some time. Her people, as has been remarked, were mostly Americans who had come in there. All their

TEXAS

political ideas were American. They were of what we may call, for the sake of a name, the Anglo-Saxon race; while the Mexicans were of another stock. They could have no sympathy with Mexican ideas and politics. It was natural for them to turn to us, as it was natural for us to sympathise with them. Their only tie to Mexico was political. Texas was everything she should not be to make Mexican sovereignty suitable or acceptable. The objection to annexation lay in the time of the act and the surrounding circumstances. It meant, in all probability and apparently designedly, a war with Mexico which had been at peace with us. It was a direct act of aggression, however extenuating the failure of Mexico to reconquer the revolted district may have been. The object appeared to many to be not to help a people near of kin to us and our institutions, but through a war of conquest to acquire territory to be devoted to slavery. Mexico's possession meant freedom for the negro, while ours meant slavery. As Henry Clay writes in December, 1844, " The Whigs were most anxious to avoid a foreign war for the sake of acquiring a foreign territory, which, under the circumstances of the acquisition, could not fail to produce domestic discord and expose the character of the country, in the eyes of an impartial world, to severe animadversion."

CHAPTER VIII.

THE MEXICAN CESSION.

ALTHOUGH the Mexican government announced that it would maintain its right to Texas by force of arms, and all attempts at diplomatic arrangement failed, no outbreak of hostilities occurred until the next year. It seems very much as if the United States were bent on war, and a war of conquest at that. She took the quarrel of Texas directly upon her own shoulders. Besides committing an act of war against Mexico by annexing Texas, she also by so doing, involved herself in a dispute over the boundary of that State, and pushed her claims to the utmost limit. Mexico claimed the river Nueces as the western limit, while the United States claimed the land to the Rio Grande. By carrying the boundary to that river, we really annexed a large strip of territory on which neither an American nor Texan had made a single settlement, and which included a part of the Mexican State of New Mexico. Texas grew in size very rapidly from the time she was a part of Mexico to the time of her annexation to the United States.

TERRITORIAL ACQUISITIONS

When Texas agreed to the annexation, "the President was requested and authorised to lose no time in establishing a line of frontier posts and occupying any exposed portion along the western border of the new State," and General Taylor was sent to Texas with an army of occupation. He halted in a position north of the Nueces River, and hoisted the American flag. Early in 1846 he was ordered to the Rio Grande; and, when he crossed the Nueces to carry out his orders, he entered the disputed territory. This was looked upon by Mexico as a still further invasion of her land,— even if she had given up Texas, which she had not,— and a force of Mexican dragoons attacked a small body of our men. This was enough for President Polk and the party in power. We remember that Jefferson had not been so hasty forty years before. On May 11, 1846, war was declared; and the unequal struggle began. Unequal because the Mexican armies, no matter how much they might outnumber ours, no matter that they were fighting for their own country, in sight of their own homes, were always beaten. Unequal especially, because the government behind them was weak, distracted by constant

THE MEXICAN CESSION

rebellions, a mere shadow. To add to Mexico's difficulties, our government practically stirred up a revolution in Mexican government, in the midst of the war, by opening a way for Santa Anna — who had been driven into exile before the war began — to return to Mexico, and really inducing him to do so. It was doubtless calculated that Mexico, embroiled afresh in domestic difficulties, would be a still easier prey for the United States, and that Santa Anna, in return, would favour the ultimate designs of this country. But he disappointed these expectations. Probably he found that a vigourous resistance to American aggression was the surest road to popularity; and, when he got to Mexico and seized the reins of power, our advance was more vigourously contested than before. Benton, in his "Thirty Years' View," thus characterises these intrigues : —

"What must history say of the policy and morality of such doings? The butcher of American prisoners at Goliad, San Patricio, the Old Mission, and the Alamo; the destroyer of republican government at home; the military dictator, aspiring to permanent supreme power,— this man to be restored to power by the United States, for the purpose

TERRITORIAL ACQUISITIONS

of fulfilling speculations and indemnity calculations on which the war was begun!"

The United States very early made propositions of peace. Nothing came of them, so far as Mexico was concerned; but here a collateral question was raised, which lasted so long as the cause of that war. A bill was introduced into Congress to authorise the President to use three million dollars as he deemed it expedient in negotiating a treaty of peace with Mexico. To this an amendment was offered, known as the Wilmot Proviso, prohibiting slavery in any territory to be acquired under that treaty or in any way whatsoever. The bill, with the proviso, passed the House, but did not reach the Senate in time to pass that session. It was the beginning of the end of slavery. That proviso was notice that a large and increasing number of the people were opposed to any further extension of slavery. "It announced a policy which was afterward to be victorious."

The war went on until General Scott entered the City of Mexico. That settled the contest. The treaty of Guadalupe Hidalgo, concluded Feb. 2, 1848, defined the terms of peace; and the war was ended. As a result, besides confirming our title to Texas,

THE MEXICAN CESSION

Mexico ceded to the United States California and all the country between that district and Texas which we own to-day except a little strip ceded to us in 1853. The same stipulation in regard to the people of the country ceded was incorporated in the treaty, as in the case of Louisiana, except that the provision was added that Congress should be the sole judge of the propriety of the admission of new States formed from the new territory. Practically, the United States agreed to form States from that territory so soon as Congress deemed it proper to do so. The United States paid Mexico $15,000,000, and released her from claims of American citizens to an amount of $3,250,000, and also agreed to protect her northern boundary from the incursions and misconduct of the Indians. The war cost us in round numbers $150,000,000, and, it is said, 25,000 lives, counting the deaths which resulted in every way from it.

The glory of the Mexican War rests upon the army alone, and the common soldier is entitled to the most of it. The bravery shown by him, the dogged courage and persistent effort and intelligence, were the same as have characterised the American soldier

TERRITORIAL ACQUISITIONS

from the first, and are still shown by him to-day. His general who led the way to Mexico became the next President; while the party which was responsible for the war — which had made the annexation of Texas a party principle — was utterly defeated when next the people went to the polls.

There seemed to be a prospect of further trouble with Mexico in 1853, but the Gadsden treaty settled the matter by annexing to the United States some 30,000 square miles along the southern bank of the Gila River. This territory forms the southern part of what is now New Mexico and Arizona. The difficulty all arose over a disputed boundary. The boundary commissioners set off the Mesilla Valley as belonging to Mexico, whereupon our governor of New Mexico objected, claiming that they were in error, and proceeded to take possession of the disputed territory until the boundary could be settled by the United States and Mexico. Mexico protested; and, since Santa Anna was at the head of the government and unfriendly to us, matters looked somewhat stormy. But a settlement was effected by which this strip was ceded to the United States, and the latter released from

THE MEXICAN CESSION

the obligation to protect Mexico's northern boundary from the Indians. In return the United States paid Mexico $10,000,000.

This acquisition from Mexico marks our last acquisition of contiguous territory. The annexation of Texas and the land ceded to us by Mexico contained nearly a million square miles in territory, but outside of Texas very sparsely inhabited, very much of it almost unknown. California began to grow with the discovery of its gold mines after its acquisition by us. For the purpose for which the war was undertaken the results seem to answer; and yet, in spite of any material advantage gained, the Texan and Mexican business is hardly to our credit. It was very much like the case of a powerful neighbour taking a piece of land he wanted from a weaker neighbour, and paying for it what he pleased. Yet the results even in a moral and political point of view were not wholly undesirable. The Mexican War and the annexation of Texas marked the extreme power of the slave-holding interest at the South, and the exercise of that power solidified the opposition North and West. The institution of slavery, although it seemed at the time to be reinvigorated, really received

TERRITORIAL ACQUISITIONS

its death-blow then; any seeming advance which it made then or thereafter was at the expense of a support which it required to exist. Texas was the last slave State to be admitted to the Union. "What the Abolitionists could not do, the slaveholders and their adherents did by opening the eyes of the people and showing them how near they were to the brink of the precipice."

The same impulses which drove this country in its course with Mexico were active for some time afterward in efforts to gain additional territory at the South. These efforts lasted until the Civil War ended slavery; but private attempts to acquire some of the West Indies or parts of Central America, during that time, ended in disaster and failure, and official intrigues fared no better. Then came the Civil War, as a consequence of the disease in our system which led to the Mexican War; and we were too busy in trying to build up a new government or saving the Union to think of annexing foreign lands.

CHAPTER IX.
ALASKA.

AFTER the Civil War we bought Alaska. Up to this point, in the history of our acquisitions, we have found that political necessities or advantages, actual or alleged, have been the reasons for annexation. In the case of Alaska it was mainly financial or commercial reasons. Alaska was a country which did not touch our boundaries at any point. Although sparsely inhabited except by the natives, from its geographical location and its climate it offered no inducements for a large emigration of our people or of Europeans. In other words, while every other addition to our territory would, in the ordinary course of growth, become States, this Alaska purchase "offered little or no prospect of ever becoming fit for admission to the Union on an equal footing with the States." And it is questionable whether the recent discovery of gold will make any material change in the permanent condition of things in that respect.

In annexing Alaska, the United States took another step in the direction of acquiring any

TERRITORIAL ACQUISITIONS

territory, wherever situated, the only question being as to the benefit to be derived from the step. To be sure, the Civil War, just ended, had made the executive and Congress high-handed. It had stretched executive power and the federal power to an extreme limit. Its effect had been to centralise power in the federal government; and, with Louisiana and Texas in its memory, the latter found little difficulty in assuming a power to buy Alaska. It is needless to say that the consent of its few civilised inhabitants or its natives was no more asked than in any previous case, except that of Texas, where the original proposition of annexation came from that people. And in this connection, with the fact that the natural expectation was that Alaska should remain under a territorial form of government or be governed directly by the President and Congress, it should not be forgotten that a territorial form of government is practically the government of a colony. The government does not rest upon the consent of the governed. And, while in all previous cases such a condition of affairs was to be but a temporary expedient, and the form of government adopted in most cases allowed enough

ALASKA

local self-government to familiarise all the people with it and with the principles of the future State government, in Alaska it was expected to be permanent. Whether this is in accordance with the spirit of our institutions or not is not to be discussed here. In Alaska the circumstances, geographical or otherwise, of the territory, should be considered. But the question is raised, if, under our Constitution, we may hold communities, because of geographical or climatic conditions likely to keep the number of inhabitants small, under a sort of colonial government,— government from Washington and not from themselves,— may we not also hold them in this way because of peculiarities or characteristics in the population?

Alaska is our name for the Russian possessions in America ceded to us in 1867. Russia's title was that of discovery. Bering, in the service of that country, after he found out in 1728 that Asia and North America were not connected by land, started in 1741 on another voyage of discovery. On July 18 of that year " he sighted a rocky range of coast, behind which towered lofty mountains, their summits white with perpetual snows," and thus caught his first glimpse

TERRITORIAL ACQUISITIONS

of what was afterward known as Russian America. The Russians were soon active in exploration. Search was made for a northeast passage to the Atlantic, and mercantile adventurers examined the coast and islands. In 1783 Russian companies began the fur trade, afterward participated in to some extent by Americans. Russia, however, did not penetrate far inland. The Hudson's Bay Company were already in the field in the interior. In 1825 a treaty fixed the line between British and Russian possessions, while the year before (1824) Russia, by treaty with the United States, as stated awhile ago, fixed her southern limit at the parallel of 54° 40′. She also granted to our people certain fishing privileges; but her government so construed the compact as to exclude our vessels from just the places to which they wanted to go, where the fishing was known to be the best.

It was the desire of the Pacific Coast for additional privileges that brought about the treaty of 1867, which gave us the whole country. The cod-fishing carried on by vessels from San Francisco had become by that year quite an industry. In 1865 one of the officials of Washington Territory reported the abundance of cod and halibut in this region of Alaska, and said: "No one who knows these facts for a moment doubts that, if vessels used by the Bank fishermen that sail from Massachusetts and Maine were fitted out here and were to fish on the various banks along this coast, it would even now be a most lucrative business." The legislature of that same territory, by formal resolution, called the attention of the general government to the great value of the fisheries of the Russian American coast, and petitioned for the adoption of such measures as would obtain for Americans the right to fish in these waters. The desire to obtain fishing-grounds in the western waters, as well as in the eastern, and to gain them free from the entanglements of those in the East, and possibly a desire to have another naval station on the Pacific, as President Johnson in a message to Congress suggested, must have been controlling factors in the mind of the administration in making the treaty, to say nothing of the value of the fur and seal industry. The mineral wealth was of a decidedly uncertain character.

Russia was quite willing to dispose of her holdings in America. These possessions

TERRITORIAL ACQUISITIONS

would be hard to defend in case of war, especially with England; and yet it would be at least annoying to lose them through war. They afforded no strength to her, but were rather a weakness. Then she wanted the money. So the transfer was easily brought about. It is quite possible that our own difficulties with the reconstruction problems at the time distracted the interest of the public in the transaction, for the treaty ceding the country to us, made March 29, 1867, occasioned very little discussion, and was ratified with substantial equanimity on April 9. When we came to pay over the cash called for by the treaty, there was a little delay. It seemed to many quite a lot of money for a purchase of doubtful value. Congress finally appropriated the amount; and it was charged, but not proven, that quite a corruption fund was necessary to effect this. It is true, however, that a very respectable sum was used in writing up the country in favourable terms.

We paid $7,250,000 for it, and acquired about 580,000 square miles of territory, inhabited by some 60,000 people, mostly Esquimaux,— a native population which, like that of our Indians, is diminishing in its contact with civilization. The treaty pro-

ALASKA

vided that such of the civilised inhabitants as remained in Alaska were to have all the rights of citizens of the United States.

With this acquisition the United States has, up to this time, remained content so far as any territory on or adjacent to this continent is concerned. The power of our government to annex foreign territory seems to be pretty well established by precedent; but, with the exception of Texas,— which, however, had a population in which the American element was largely predominant,— all our acquisitions, up to the time of and including Alaska, were of sparsely settled countries. Louisiana was no exception; for nearly all its population was clustered round New Orleans, leaving an immense space inhabited almost wholly by Indians. Outside of Alaska the acquisitions have opened outlets for immigration from the older States and from abroad; and the new territories have become American in thought and institutions because the pioneers in all these new countries were largely Americans. "They have been a leaven in the European immigration which followed. The two elements, acting together, have built up communities capable of taking a place among the self-governing States."

TERRITORIAL ACQUISITIONS

Whether Alaska be considered an exception, from its peculiar location and from the circumstances which seemed to make its acquisition desirable, or whether it be considered as an established precedent, the recent steps in the enlargement of our territory are certainly of a different character from any which have gone before. These acquisitions of to-day show that, admitting our constitutional power to acquire territory, we professedly are guided now by different reasons from those in the old days, when our country was younger.

CHAPTER X.
HAWAII.

THIRTY-ONE years elapsed after the purchase of Alaska before we entered upon a new career of territorial expansion; and we began by annexing the Hawaiian Islands. In doing this, we took a long step forward, admitting that we can find authority for so doing in the earlier precedents. Since it marks something of a departure from our course of action up to this point, a somewhat more extended account of the causes which resulted in this annexation seems desirable. Whereas all the former acquisitions had been of territory which seemed suitable for emigration of our people or presented commercial advantages, Hawaii offers little field for emigration, for in 1890 only 4,695 persons owned the land, and more than half the soil had passed into European or American hands; and it would seem that most, if not all, the commercial benefits might have been obtained by a close alliance or protectorate. To be sure, political reasons prompted the acquisition of Louisiana and Florida, and indeed, of Texas and the land gained from

TERRITORIAL ACQUISITIONS

Mexico; but still the land gained was open, and suitable for emigration. In the case of Hawaii this fact is not present; and political reasons alone governed the action taken. In fact, the annexation was justified on naval grounds or to protect the American interests, already paramount in the islands.

The annexation was not accomplished without opposition, and in the end was helped, if not carried through, by supposed necessities arising out of the situation in which we found ourselves in the early part of our war with Spain in 1898. It was really the pressure of a small but energetic minority of American residents and sympathisers in Hawaii, rather than the wish of the United States, that inaugurated and maintained the movement which led to annexation.

The Hawaiian Islands are a country two thousand miles away from our coast, and had in 1897 a population of 109,020, of which only 5,336 were Americans or British, and 39,504 native or half Hawaiians, who held at least a nominal share in the government. Portuguese, Germans, Japanese and Chinese made up the rest of the mixed population,— the Japanese and Chinese, to the number of 46,023, having no part in the government actual or nominal.

Loving political freedom as we do, and with our own inborn energy, somehow we have a feeling of compassion, mingled with a tinge of impatience, as we read the history of these islands since Captain Cook discovered them in 1778, three years after we had begun the fight for our own independence. The people are a race redeemed from barbarism. Mr. Schouler speaks of the native Hawaiian as "timid to resist the encroachments of a more powerful race, docile without strong traditions of his own, frail, but well-intentioned in morals"; and another refers to him as possessing, to an unusual degree, a capacity for fine and ardent enthusiasm for noble ends. The gentle Hawaiians show the distinctive Christian traits, " not always predominant among their more civilised teachers, of simple faith, meekness, self-sacrificing hospitality, and forgiveness of their enemies by whom they have suffered." More than half of them can read and write,— a showing which should particularly commend them to us, especially since this moral and intellectual growth was planted and fostered by American mission-

TERRITORIAL ACQUISITIONS

aries. And we should not forget that it was under native rulers that this uplifting began and was continued. We must feel a sympathy for them as we see how their own government came more and more under the influence and control of foreign residents, chiefly Americans, until the native Hawaiians were relegated to a very subordinate place in their own country. As the Indian here is disappearing before the civilisation of his conquerors, so the Hawaiian is fading away under the protection of the aliens he admitted to his home.

When Captain Cook was there, the islands were ruled by separate chiefs independent of each other; but one of them by his superior ability subdued all the islands except two, which yielded their allegiance to his successor. The first Hawaiian king, as Kamehameha I., began a dynasty which lasted until the death of Kamehameha V. in 1874 without a successor. The interference by the French in 1837 led to a formal declaration of independence in 1840 and the promulgation of a constitution by Kamehameha III. The independence of the islands was recognised in 1844 by England and the United States. Christianity had been intro-

HAWAII

duced by Kamehameha II.; and the disposition of the islanders was such that the Christian religion made rapid progress, and, with occasional relapses, it has maintained its hold upon them. The influence of the missionary is seen all through these earlier days; and the influence of his descendants, not wholly directed toward the religious welfare of the natives, has been almost equally strong.

Again, in 1849, new complications with the French occurred; and hostile preparations were begun, which were interrupted only upon the protests of the English and American representatives. When once again, in 1851, the French threatened hostilities, the king, Kamehameha III., found it advisable to strengthen his alliance with the United States; and, acting upon the advice of American missionaries and American residents, he promulgated a new constitution, admitting a small number of foreigners to each of the two houses of the legislature. Annexation to the United States even then was discussed, but afterward abandoned.

When Kamehameha V. died, in 1874, without a successor, the legislature, chiefly through external American influence, elected

TERRITORIAL ACQUISITIONS

as king, Kalakaua, one of the royal house, over the dowager queen Emma, a daughter of an English physician. In Kalakaua's reign, in 1876, a treaty of reciprocity was arranged with the United States, which developed a marvellous interchange of products on our Pacific coast. The broadening of commerce arising from this act carried to Hawaii a large "amount of American invested capital, together with a fair colony of sojourners more or less constant" from this country.

Kalakaua's course as king was hardly on a par with that of his predecessors; and his dissipation and his government produced a revolution in 1887, which secured a constitution so liberal in its treatment of the white residents as to be, to use Mr. Schouler's words, "unparalleled in the dealings of civilised nations with aliens." Under that constitution procured by the white residents, foreigners who took the oath to support the Hawaiian government were permitted to register as voters with a distinct reservation of allegiance to their own governments. Under it a citizen of the United States could remain such, and still have the right to vote in Hawaiian elections, while he was a resident, by simply swearing to support the government.

HAWAII

It deprived the sovereign of his absolute veto upon legislation, and took away from him his power under the old constitution of appointing the members of the Upper House. Naturally, actual power passed to the foreign residents, if they kept in accord. In practice the successive kings had appointed white men as ministers, nobles, and judges, in preference to men of their own race, while sons of missionaries and the English-speaking residents in general had always occupied high places and reaped very satisfactory pecuniary benefits. With this position already gained, the new constitution made this class still more powerful, as it was also the more aggressive.

Matters stood in this way when, in 1891, Kalakaua died while on a tour to the United States, where American interests saw to it that he was entertained right royally. Liliuokalani, his sister and successor, was proclaimed queen; and almost immediately schemes for annexation to the United States began to be formed.

The foreign sojourners — American citizens still, for the most part — became intensely anxious, in the interest of a stable government and of their own pecuniary concerns as well, that the government of the United States should be extended over the islands; while the white residents there, the descendants of missionaries and of officials, naturally preferred a union with a strong government like our own to a possible resumption of power by the natives. They wanted above all a stable government; and if their sympathies with the annexation movement were not so strong, they were not bitterly opposed to it.

The new queen, Liliuokalani, had an even stronger dislike than her predecessor for the constitution forced upon him in 1887; and she was a less pliable subject than he. Passionate and high-strung as she was, with a strong love for her native subjects and loved by them, with a large native vote which, if it could all be brought out, might swamp the foreign vote, there was a danger that the power of the white residents might become less secure; and the alien population recognized the danger. The queen found herself merely a figure-head in the government, a situation she could hardly abide. Her disposition was reactionary, and her sympathies entirely with her native people. She had at least inklings of the design to annex her

HAWAII

whole kingdom to the country whose citizens within her own dominion held a good share of the actual power. With such a woman (of little tact and headstrong in dispute) as queen, the annexation feeling grew stronger, until her own imprudence and folly threw the key of the situation into her opponents' hands.

CHAPTER XI.

HAWAII (Concluded).

On Jan. 14, 1893, the legislature was prorogued, not to meet again until May, 1894, having at the last moment turned out of office a ministry favoured by the reformers and the foreign element. The new ministry thus put in power, which must remain in power until a new legislature should meet, stood for nothing except personal and political success, so far as we can see. Politics in Hawaii did not seem to be all that could be desired. Charges of corruption were freely made, and personal intrigue was apparent in the doings of the legislature. The new ministry, in fulfilling pledges probably given to the combination in the legislature which had put them in power, laid before the queen two measures, offensive to our people, but favoured by some local interests there,—a lottery act and an opium license act. The queen, although disliking the acts, affixed her signature to them because she wanted something from the ministry in turn. It was unfortunate for her that she did so, for it gave her opponents a chance to take "the high moral" ground against her; but we cannot help feeling that, however strong their opposition to these acts was, the annexationists cared more for her action in the matter as an argument against her than for the principle involved. Having signed the bills, the queen brought forward her scheme. Urged by her own people and her own inclinations, but in practical defiance of the whole foreign element, with a self-reliance which would have been admirable had it not been so indiscreet, she submitted a new constitution, which she wished immediately proclaimed in place of that of 1887. It was not such an extremely reactionary document. It practically put the supreme law back where it was before the revolution of 1887, but it proposed one or two changes which would necessarily be opposed by the white residents. The queen wished to take away the life tenure of the judiciary, and, most sweeping change of all, to reduce the property qualification for the suffrage, and provide that only subjects should vote. We can hardly blame her for desiring that last step.

The ministry saw that it would not do. Although the right of the sovereign to proclaim a new constitution strictly followed precedent, the changes suggested would produce a revolution in any event. They struck down the safeguards of the rich and intelligent foreign element, whose presence and capital had made the prosperity of the whole community. Even the queen felt bound to gain her ministry's consent to promulgate the document; and, when she failed to obtain that, she submitted. "With heartfelt sorrow and yet queenly self-control" she announced to the Hawaiians from her royal balcony that, while she loved her people and would continue to love them, she could not then give them the constitution they wished for, but would do so some time. Even in this she yielded to her ministry after long discussion during the rest of the day, and abandoned in full her purpose at any time to make the wished for changes; and on the forenoon of the following Monday, January 16, public announcement of that fact was made over her own signature.

It would seem, therefore, that any need of resistance to her authority on account of her proposed action, now forever abandoned, was obviated; but the zealous annexationists seized upon the opportunity to effect their

HAWAII

purpose. The foreign residents assembled in mass meeting and appointed a Committee of Safety with discretionary powers. This committee, on January 16, issued a proclamation abrogating the monarchical system and establishing a provisional government, consisting of an Executive Council of four "to exist until terms of union with the United States of America have been negotiated and acted upon." The council at once assumed control of the government, and obliged the queen to retire to her private residence; and all this was accomplished without bloodshed. About the only force visible was a body of marines landed from an American war vessel in the harbour of Honolulu. It is needless to say that this provisional government represented the foreign, and particularly, the American element at Hawaii. Commissioners of this government were hurried off to Washington to negotiate a treaty of annexation, and they found there an almost suspiciously favourable reception.

The unfortunate part which the United States played in this revolution was the all too prompt recognition of the new government by the resident United States minister at Honolulu, and the landing of American marines, at his request, ostensibly to protect American interests, but practically to compel submission to the new order of things. Well may the queen complain that, but for the attitude of the accredited minister of a friendly nation, her government might have continued to exist. It cannot be doubted, from a review of the facts, that it was the marine force from our war-ship which made the bloodless revolution successful.

A treaty of annexation was concluded by President Harrison's administration and, with a favourable recommendation, laid by him before the Senate on February 15, but later was withdrawn from that body by President Cleveland without action upon it having been taken. President Cleveland sent a commissioner to the Hawaiian Islands to investigate, and his message to Congress, upon receiving the commissioner's report, shows his own conviction of the injustice to the Hawaiians committed in assisting the revolution with our troops. Yet political conditions here, the rancour of party feeling, the appeals to a false pride, and, above all, the situation into which affairs at Honolulu had grown, made a solution of the problem difficult. Secretary Gresham's plan,

HAWAII

as outlined in his report, favouring a restoration of the political conditions which existed in Hawaii previous to the revolution, so far as United States troops had assisted in that revolution, was attended with almost insuperable objections. All that the President could do was to withdraw the protectorate over Hawaii which Minister Stevens had established on February 9, pending action by Congress on the treaty of annexation; and this was done on April 14, 1893.

On July 4, 1894, the provisional government was dissolved, and a republic proclaimed. The movement for annexation was then more vigourously carried on than before; and on June 16, 1897, another treaty of annexation was sent to the Senate by President McKinley. But this was never acted upon. After that we became involved in war with Spain, and, as one result of that, joint resolutions providing for the annexation of Hawaii passed Congress, and were approved by President McKinley, July 7, 1898.

The war with Spain, like all other wars, was attended by unexpected results. Whatever may have been in the minds of our public men, certainly in the minds of the

TERRITORIAL ACQUISITIONS

people of this country there was no other idea in the early part of 1898 than to free Cuba from Spanish control,—to end the bloodshed and scandal of misrule at our doors. When effecting that object brought us into war with Spain, and when, in the course of that war, Puerto Rico and Manila fell into our hands, a new thought forced itself into the minds of many of our people, a new vision of the future spread itself before their eyes. No longer, with the weakness of youth, would we shelter ourselves behind our ocean barriers, but with the strength of a young manhood we would take up our part in redeeming the world from barbarism. With such views developing in the popular mind, it was easy for the ardent annexationists of Hawaii and the United States to persuade what had hitherto been a reluctant people to consent to a union with Hawaii, to take advantage of our own wrong-doing. For it was alleged with considerable vigour that those islands were a needed station on the route to the far-off Philippines, and that, if we were to hold sway at Manila, we scarcely could do without Hawaii. Looking at it in this way, the acquisition of the Hawaiian Islands is a part

HAWAII

only of a scheme of expansion upon which we have entered, and the supposed necessity of the acquisition may justify the departure from all our traditions which such annexation involves.

I do not need to enlarge upon the problems brought to us by this annexation, difficult and unusual with us as they are. With Hawaii we indeed entered upon a new career; and, in addition to solving the problem of just and decent government at home, — by no means yet finished,— we have taken upon our shoulders the government of new and strange people. Still, the annexation having been accomplished, it behooves us to meet the difficulties as wisely and as best we can.

CHAPTER XII.
CONCLUSION.

I HAVE dwelt at considerable length upon this Hawaiian annexation, because, in addition to its being a new departure in our history, it is so closely connected with the policy which we are pursuing in regard to acquiring territories in the West Indies and the East. It is not my purpose to enter into any discussion of these latter enlargements of the territory covered by our flag. Their story is fresh in our minds; and, with Hawaii, they make another chapter in our history, quite different from what has gone before.

In every acquisition, up to those of Puerto Rico and the Philippines, it has been our own interest which has been consulted. Now we are entering upon a career of acquisition for ostensibly a different set of reasons,— the benefit of the people brought under our dominion; and Hawaii was a step in aid of that object. It is not for me in this place to say where we shall or should stop, nor do I wish to speak of the advantages or disadvantages to ourselves of such a course.

CONCLUSION

The result of this review of our past shows us, I believe, that our country has grown not only in territory, but in the power of its federal government to extend its sphere and enlarge its boundaries in whatever direction it deems proper. There has been hardly a year since the acquisition of Louisiana, certainly not since the Mexican War, when the annexation of some island or country has not been proposed or discussed by some of our public men. Cuba, San Domingo, Hayti, and countries in Central America, all have been considered in that connection. It is only in the cases told of in these pages where public sentiment or particular circumstances have brought about a union with our country. It has come to be, not a question of the constitutional power to acquire territory, but the desirability of its acquisition in each particular case. It is for us, the people, to say how far this extension of power shall go and how far we shall feel that we have the strength, or that it is our duty, to carry the benefits of our institutions. Others may sound the note of warning or exhort to further efforts: I have tried only to tell what we have done in the past, and why.

The story of our acquisitions of territory

TERRITORIAL ACQUISITIONS

is not all creditable to us. It shows us that the type of humanity which our institutions have evolved has been ready, as have the powers of the Old World, in the name of our country to wrong other people weaker than ourselves. This has been partly through ignorance of the real facts; but the past should teach us to be on our guard to prevent future actions by the Executive and Congress which are contrary to our professions. The story of our acquisitions shows one thing clearly, that we have acquired foreign territory whenever and wherever we have considered it an advantage to do so, and the consent of the people affected has not been asked. It is too late to doubt the power of our government, under our Constitution to-day, to do so. Whether we wish to limit that power in the future is an entirely different matter. If the people wish to make such a limitation, they can do so. Our great duty now is to consider well the acquisitions we do make, and to treat in accordance with the ideals and principles which have animated our truest patriots and wisest statesmen the people who come under our flag. If these people are not fitted to be citizens of self-governing States, all the more

CONCLUSION

do we hold their welfare and happiness and development in our hands; and our duty to them is a trust we cannot abuse if we would be true to our ideals and the hopes of humanity.

APPENDIX

APPENDIX

SCHEDULE I.

Showing the Territory and Population acquired since the Grant of the Northwestern Territory.

Geographical name.	Area, square miles.	Population at date of acquisition.	Population in 1890.	States and Territories now comprised within the boundaries of the acquisitions.
Louisiana purchase in 1802	864,931	80,000	11,000,000	Arkansas, Indian Territory, Iowa, Missouri, Nebraska, No. Dakota, So. Dakota, nearly whole of Louisiana, greater parts of Kansas, Minnesota, Montana, and Wyoming, and parts of Colorado and Oklahoma.
Florida purchase in 1819	59,268	4,000	600,000	Florida and small parts of Alabama, Louisiana, and Mississippi.
Oregon, portion set off to United States in 1846	307,000	12,000	770,000	Idaho, Oregon, Washington, and small parts of Montana and Wyoming.

APPENDIX

Texas annexation in 1845	375,239	150,000	2,300,000	Texas, and small parts of Colorado, Kansas, New Mexico, and Oklahoma.
Mexican cessions in 1846 and 1853	591,318	80,000	1,600,000	Arizona, California, Nevada, Utah, parts of Colorado and New Mexico, and small part of Wyoming.
Alaska purchase in 1867	577,390	60,000	30,000	Alaska.
Hawaiian annexation in 1898	6,582	109,020	—	Hawaii.
Spanish cession, 1899: Porto Rico Philippine Islands Guam	3,550 114,326 300	806,708 6,990,000 8,000	— — —	Porto Rico. Philippine Islands. Guam.

APPENDIX

SCHEDULE II.

COMPARATIVE AREA OF UNITED STATES AND ITS ACQUISITIONS, AND OF CERTAIN EUROPEAN COUNTRIES.

United States and Acquisitions.	Area, square miles.	European Countries.	Area, square miles.
United States in 1783	827,844	Austria-Hungary, German Empire, France, and Sweden	826,720
Louisiana purchase	864,931	Austria-Hungary, German Empire, France, Sweden, Switzerland, and Greece	867,678
Florida purchase	59,268	England and Wales	58,310
Oregon partition	307,000	Italy and Spain	308,316

APPENDIX

Texas annexation	375,239	Austria-Hungary, Great Britain, and Denmark	377,184
Mexican cessions	591,318	German Empire, France, and Spain	610,592
Alaska	577,390	German Empire, France, and Norway	585,798
United States, 1867 to 1898	3,602,990	All Europe except Norway and Sweden	3,689,654
Hawaii and Spanish cessions, 1898–99	124,758	Great Britain	120,979
United States, 1899	3,727,748	All Europe except Austria-Hungary	3,746,053

APPENDIX

SCHEDULE III.

COMPARATIVE POPULATION OF UNITED STATES WITH CERTAIN EUROPEAN COUNTRIES.

United States.	Population.	European Countries.	Population.
United States in 1783	3,929,214	Scotland in 1891	4,033,103
United States in 1898	*74,500,000	German Empire, Spain, and Portugal in 1898 †	74,895,276
United States in 1899	*85,000,000	German Empire and Italy †	83,570,405

* Estimate.   † Not including colonies.

www.ingramcontent.com/pod-product-compliance
Lightning Source LLC
Chambersburg PA
CBHW021918180426

43199CB00032B/704